THE

Norton Anthology
of Modern Poetry

THE

Norton Anthology

of Modern Poetry

EDITED BY

RICHARD ELLMANN

Goldsmiths' Professor of English Literature, Oxford University

AND

ROBERT O'CLAIR

Professor of English, Manhattanville College

W · W · NORTON & COMPANY

New York · London

COPYRIGHT © 1973 BY W. W. NORTON & COMPANY, INC.

Library of Congress Cataloging in Publication Data
Ellmann, Richard, 1918–   comp.
  The Norton anthology of modern poetry.

  Bibliography.
    1. American poetry—20th century.   2. English
poetry.   3. American poetry—19th century.   4. English
poetry—19th century.   I. O'Clair, Robert, joint comp.
II. Title.
PS323.5.E5   1973   821'.008   73–6587

W. W. Norton & Company, Inc. 500 Fifth Avenue, New York, N.Y. 10110

Published simultaneously in Canada by Stoddart,
a subsidiary of General Publishing Co. Ltd.,
Don Mills, Ontario.

PRINTED IN THE UNITED STATES OF AMERICA

4 5 6 7 8 9

ISBN 0-393-09357-3 CL
ISBN 0-393-09348-4 PBK

Preface

The most acute rendering of an era's sensibility is its poetry. In the twentieth century, probably in reaction to its horrors, poets have created new and powerful consolidations of the imaginative life. Some writers have accepted the discipline of the literary tradition, others have flouted it. During the last seventy-five years in the English-speaking nations, many poets of consequence have written well in an unprecedented range of styles and subjects. This book aspires to present their best work, and also to delineate the many different tendencies of modern poetry in English.

Where to begin a selection of modern verse is a problem that has been solved here by the inclusion of four earlier poets—Walt Whitman first, and then Emily Dickinson, Gerard Manley Hopkins, and Thomas Hardy. These poets either anticipate or influence much verse that came after them. We have chosen to present them, and all modern poets, not according to nationality—though many prided themselves on their national origins—but in terms of generations. For in the twentieth century, distinctions of age more often appear to create boundaries than do places of composition. The history of verse in England cannot be written without considering Pound and Eliot, both born in the United States, while in the history of American verse it has to be noted that Whitman, and Robert Frost after him, found their most sympathetic early audiences in England, and that W. H. Auden, having made his reputation as an English poet, in middle life became a citizen of the United States.

In this book, we have included many poems by each major figure, but we have also provided a generous selection of poets less celebrated but still of commanding interest. This procedure seems preferable to offering the major writers by themselves, since it situates them within the context in which they wrote and were read. It is preferable also to a miscellaneous survey in which all poets are presented through a perfunctory sampling. We have also gathered here in considerable abundance the poetry written since the Second World War, which is so often slighted in collections of this kind. Excellent poems are still being written, and we have tried to suggest their vitality and range. Of course, a choice had to be made among many good poems; doubtless there are not only some poems but some poets that readers may miss, but we hope that few will find this book completely lacking in the *kind* of modern poetry in which they are specially interested.

A book of modern verse bears a responsibility to assist readers who might be put off by the profusion of talent, on the one hand, or by the range of allusion and local reference on the other. Most such collections have been chary of footnotes, even those by the poets themselves, yet the intelligibility of a line, or even a poem, often depends on specialized knowledge. We have provided liberal annotation, translating phrases from foreign languages and explaining allusions when they are not common knowledge, so that every poem can be read without re-

course to reference books. The introductions which preface the selections from each poet attempt to place them in relation to others, as well as to provide a sense of what they wished their work to accomplish. The bibliography will help readers eager to pursue particular poets.

A note about texts: as a general rule, we have given the latest published version of a poem over which the author could have exercised editorial control. Certain exceptions have been made, and these are identified in the footnotes; occasionally lines from an alternative version of a poem are also given. Except where the sequence would be misleading, poems are arranged under each author in the order of their first appearance in book form, and the date of that publication is specified after each poem. For convenience, poems without titles are usually identified by their first lines, which are given in square brackets in the table of contents and above the poem itself. Almost all the poems are printed in their entirety, but a few very long ones have had to be represented by self-contained selections, their omitted portions being indicated by three asterisks. Individualities of spelling, punctuation, and typography have been preserved.

This book has profited greatly from the assistance of friends. We especially wish to thank Professor M. H. Abrams, both avuncular and exigent; Margaret Neussendorfer, who aided in the preparation of the texts; John Benedict, John Francis, and their colleagues at W. W. Norton & Company, Inc., for careful and benevolent editing. The resources and services of the Yale and Harvard university libraries, the Bodleian, and the Manhattanville College Library have been invaluable. We thank Mary Ellmann, who wrote the headnote on Sylvia Plath and contributed to other headnotes, and Margaret O'Clair, who helped select certain of the poems.

Contents

Preface   xiii
Introduction   1

WALT WHITMAN (1819–1892)   19
  Crossing Brooklyn Ferry   23
  Are You the New Person Drawn Toward Me?   27
  I Saw in Louisiana a Live-Oak Growing   27
  To a Stranger   27
  Cavalry Crossing a Ford   28
  By the Bivouac's Fitful Flame   28
  A Sight in Camp in the Daybreak Gray and Dim   28
  Long, Too Long America   29
  Respondez!   29
  Whispers of Heavenly Death   31
  To a Locomotive in Winter   32
  The Dismantled Ship   32

EMILY DICKINSON (1830–1886)   33
  I Shall Know Why—When Time Is Over (J. 193)   36
  There's a Certain Slant of Light (J. 258)   36
  I Breathed Enough to Take the Trick (J. 272)   36
  The Soul Selects Her Own Society (J. 303)   37
  The Difference Between Despair (J. 305)   37
  There Came a Day at Summer's Full (J. 322)   37
  I Read My Sentence—Steadily (J. 412)   38
  Much Madness Is Divinest Sense (J. 435)   38
  This Is My Letter to the World (J. 441)   38
  I Heard a Fly Buzz—When I Died (J. 465)   39
  The Brain, Within Its Groove (J. 556)   39
  The Brain—Is Wider than the Sky (J. 632)   39
  Me from Myself—to Banish (J. 642)   40
  I Dwell in Possibility (J. 657)   40
  Because I Could Not Stop for Death (J. 712)   40
  Tell All the Truth but Tell It Slant (J. 1129)   41
  There Came a Wind like a Bugle (J. 1593)   41
  The Pedigree of Honey (J. 1627)   42
  In Winter in My Room (J. 1670)   42
  My Life Closed Twice Before Its Close (J. 1732)   43

THOMAS HARDY (1840–1928)   43
  Hap   47
  Neutral Tones   47
  Drummer Hodge   47
  "I Said to Love"   48

The Subalterns   49
A Broken Appointment   49
The Darkling Thrush   50
The Respectable Burgher   51
In Tenebris: II   52
The House of Hospitalities   52
Bereft   53
Shut Out That Moon   53
1967   54
Let Me Enjoy   54
At Casterbridge Fair
   II. Former Beauties   55
New Year's Eve   55
A Young Man's Epigram on Existence   56
Channel Firing   56
The Convergence of the Twain   57
"I Found Her Out There"   58
The Voice   59
A Poet   60
In the Moonlight   60
Near Lanivet, 1872   61
The Oxen   62
In Time of "The Breaking of Nations"   62
The Blinded Bird   63
Transformations   63
"For Life I Had Never Cared Greatly"   64
Going and Staying   64
Proud Songsters   65
He Never Expected Much   65

GERARD MANLEY HOPKINS (1844–1889)   66
The Summer Malison   70
Winter with the Gulf Stream   70
Heaven-Haven   71
The Habit of Perfection   71
The Wreck of the Deutschland   72
God's Grandeur   80
Spring   80
The Windhover   81
Pied Beauty   81
Binsey Poplars   81
Duns Scotus's Oxford   82
The Bugler's First Communion   82
Felix Randal   84
Inversnaid   84
[Carrion Comfort]   85
[No Worst, There Is None. Pitched Past Pitch of Grief]   85
[I Wake and Feel the Fell of Dark, Not Day]   85
[Thou Art Indeed Just, Lord, If I Contend]   86

ROBERT BRIDGES (1844–1930)   86
London Snow   87

On a Dead Child   88
The Growth of Love
  I ("They that in play can do the thing they would")   89
  XXXIX ("A man that sees by chance his picture, made")   89
[The Snow Lies Sprinkled on the Beach]   90
Low Barometer   90

JOHN DAVIDSON (1857–1909)   91
  Thirty Bob a Week   92

A. E. HOUSMAN (1859–1936)   94
  Loveliest of Trees, the Cherry Now   97
  When I Was One-and-Twenty   97
  To an Athlete Dying Young   98
  Is My Team Ploughing   98
  Into My Heart an Air That Kills   99
  With Rue My Heart Is Laden   99
  Terence, This Is Stupid Stuff   100
  The Chestnut Casts His Flambeaux   101
  Eight O'Clock   102
  The Fairies Break Their Dances   102
  Wake Not for the World-Heard Thunder   103
  Hell Gate   103
  Epitaph on an Army of Mercenaries   105
  They Say My Verse Is Sad: No Wonder   105
  The Rainy Pleiads Wester   106
  From the Wash the Laundress Sends   106
  The Olive   106

WILLIAM BUTLER YEATS (1865–1939)   107
  The Song of the Happy Shepherd   111
  Down by the Salley Gardens   113
  To the Rose upon the Rood of Time   113
  The Lake Isle of Innisfree   114
  The Sorrow of Love   114
  When You Are Old   115
  Who Goes with Fergus?   115
  The Man Who Dreamed of Faeryland   115
  The Lamentation of the Old Pensioner   116
  To Ireland in the Coming Times   117
  The Hosting of the Sidhe   118
  Michael Robartes Bids His Beloved Be at Peace   118
  The Cap and Bells   119
  Aedh Thinks of Those Who Have Spoken Evil of His Beloved   120
  Aedh Wishes for the Cloths of Heaven   120
  In the Seven Woods   120
  Adam's Curse   121
  No Second Troy   122
  On Hearing that the Students of Our New University Have Joined
    the Agitation Against Immoral Literature   122
  Friends   122
  The Cold Heaven   123

September 1913   123
Beggar to Beggar Cried   124
The Magi   125
The Dolls   125
A Coat   126
The Wild Swans at Coole   126
The Fisherman   127
An Irish Airman Foresees His Death   128
Solomon and the Witch   128
Easter 1916   129
The Second Coming   131
A Prayer for My Daughter   132
To Be Carved on a Stone at Thoor Ballylee   133
Leda and the Swan   134
Sailing to Byzantium   134
The Tower   135
Among School Children   140
Mohini Chatterjee   142
In Memory of Eva Gore-Booth and Con Markiewicz   143
A Dialogue of Self and Soul   144
Coole Park and Ballylee, 1931   146
The Choice   147
Byzantium   147
Vacillation   148
Fragments   151
Crazy Jane Talks with the Bishop   152
Meru   152
The Gyres   153
Lapis Lazuli   153
An Acre of Grass   155
The Statues   155
News for the Delphic Oracle   156
Long-Legged Fly   157
The Circus Animals' Desertion   158
Under Ben Bulben   159

EDGAR LEE MASTERS (1868–1950)   162
The Hill   163
Cassius Hueffer   164
Amanda Barker   165
Frank Drummer   165
Fiddler Jones   165
Petit, the Poet   166
Elsa Wertman   166
Hamilton Greene   167
Editor Whedon   167
Anne Rutledge   168
Lucinda Matlock   168
Marx the Sign Painter   168
Rhoda Pitkin   169
Unknown Soldiers   169

EDWIN ARLINGTON ROBINSON (1869–1935)   170
   Luke Havergal   172
   Supremacy   172
   Calverly's   173
   How Annandale Went Out   174
   Miniver Cheevy   174
   The Companion   175
   For a Dead Lady   175
   Flammonde   176
   Cassandra   178
   John Gorham   179
   Eros Turannos   180
   Veteran Sirens   181
   The Mill   182
   The Dark Hills   182
   Tact   182
   Souvenir   183
   Firelight   183
   The New Tenants   184
   Mr. Flood's Party   184
   The Sheaves   185
   Karma   186
   As It Looked Then   186
   Reunion   186

WALTER DE LA MARE (1873–1956)   187
   The Listeners   188
   The Song of the Mad Prince   188
   A Portrait   189
   Thomas Hardy   189
   Scholars   190

ROBERT FROST (1874–1963)   190
   Mending Wall   193
   After Apple-Picking   194
   The Wood-Pile   195
   The Road Not Taken   196
   An Old Man's Winter Night   197
   The Oven Bird   197
   Birches   198
   Putting in the Seed   199
   Range-Finding   199
   The Hill Wife
     V. The Impulse   199
   The Sound of Trees   200
   The Witch of Coös   201
   Fire and Ice   204
   Stopping by Woods on a Snowy Evening   204
   For Once, Then, Something   205
   To Earthward   205
   The Need of Being Versed in Country Things   206
   Spring Pools   206

Tree at My Window   207
Acquainted with the Night   207
The Bear   208
Two Tramps in Mud Time   208
A Drumlin Woodchuck   210
Desert Places   211
Neither Out Far nor In Deep   211
Design   212
Provide, Provide   212
The Bearer of Evil Tidings   213
Never Again Would Birds' Song Be the Same   214
The Subverted Flower   214
The Gift Outright   216
Directive   216

CARL SANDBURG (1878–1967)   217
Chicago   220
Grass   220
Cool Tombs   221
Gargoyle   221
Old Timers   221
Losers   222
Aprons of Silence   223
The People, Yes
    107 ("The people will live on")   223

EDWARD THOMAS (1878–1917)   225
The Owl   227
The Path   227
When First   228
October   228
Some Eyes Condemn   229
The Green Roads   229
The Gallows   230
February Afternoon   230
The Gypsy   231

JOHN MASEFIELD (1878–1967)   231
A Consecration   233
The Everlasting Mercy (lines 1–248)   233
The Lemmings   239
The Wild Geese   239

WALLACE STEVENS (1879–1955)   242
Le Monocle de Mon Oncle   244
A High-Toned Old Christian Woman   248
The Emperor of Ice Cream   248
Anecdote of the Jar   249
Thirteen Ways of Looking at a Blackbird   249
The Idea of Order at Key West   251
The Man with the Blue Guitar
    I ("The man bent over his guitar")   252

Of Modern Poetry   253
To an Old Philosopher in Rome   253

VACHEL LINDSAY (1879–1931)   255
General William Booth Enters into Heaven   258
Abraham Lincoln Walks at Midnight   259
The Congo   260

JAMES STEPHENS (1880–1950)   264
What Tomas Said in a Pub   265
Psychometrist   265
The Rivals   266
Deirdre   266
The Paps of Dana   267
The Wind   268
A Glass of Beer   268
Egan O Rahilly   268
Sarasvati   269

JAMES JOYCE (1882–1941)   269
The Holy Office   271
[Though I Thy Mithridates Were]   273
[All Day I Hear the Noise of Waters]   274
[I Hear an Army Charging upon the Land]   274
Nightpiece   274
A Memory of the Players in a Mirror at Midnight   275
Bahnhofstrasse   275
Ecce Puer   275

ANN SPENCER (1882–   )   276
At the Carnival   276
The Wife-Woman   277

E. J. PRATT (1883–1964)   278
The Ritual   279
The Prize Cat   280
The Truant   280

WILLIAM CARLOS WILLIAMS (1883–1963)   284
Tract   288
Queen-Anne's-Lace   289
The Widow's Lament in Springtime   289
The Great Figure   290
Spring and All   290
The Eyeglasses   291
The Red Wheelbarrow   292
At the Ball Game   292
Portrait of a Lady   293
Flowers by the Sea   294
The Yachts   294
An Elegy for D. H. Lawrence   295
The Young Housewife   297
These   298

Raleigh Was Right   299
The Dance   299
Burning the Christmas Greens   299
To Ford Madox Ford in Heaven   301
Paterson
   Preface   303
   Book I, The Delineaments of the Giants
      I   ("Paterson lies in the valley . . .")   304
      I   ("They begin!")   305
     III   ("Thought clambers up")   306
Fish   307

D. H. LAWRENCE (1885–1930)   309
The Bride   312
The Enkindled Spring   312
Gloire de Dijon   312
A Youth Mowing   313
The Song of a Man Who Has Come Through   313
Piano   314
Tortoise Gallantry   314
Tortoise Shout   315
Snake   317
How Beastly the Bourgeois Is—   318
When I Went to the Circus—   320
Things Men Have Made—   322
Don'ts   322
The Elephant is Slow to Mate—   323
Red-Herring   323
When I Read Shakespeare—   324
Salt of the Earth   324
Andraitx—Pomegranate Flowers   325
The Deepest Sensuality   325
Bavarian Gentians   325
The Ship of Death   326

EZRA POUND (1885–1972)   329
Ballad of the Goodly Fere   333
Portrait d'une Femme   334
A Virginal   335
The Return   335
The River-Merchant's Wife: A Letter   336
A Pact   337
The Rest   337
In a Station of the Metro   338
The Temperaments   338
Homage to Sextus Propertius
      I   ("Shades of Callimachus, Coan ghosts of Philetas")   338
     VI   ("When, when, and whenever death closes our
         eyelids")   340
     XII   ("Who, who will be the next man to trust his girl to a
         friend?")   341
Hugh Selwyn Mauberley: Life and Contacts   343

Mauberley   351
The Cantos
    I   ("And then went down to the ship")   357
    II   ("Hang it all, Robert Browning")   539
    VII   ("Eleanor (she spoiled in a British climate)")   363
    LXXXI ("Zeus lies in Ceres' bosom")   367

H. D. (Hilda Doolittle) (1886–1961)   371
Sea Rose   373
Heat   373
Oread   373
Stars Wheel in Purple   374
The Walls Do Not Fall
    1 ("An incident here and there")   374
    4 ("There is a spell, for instance")   375
    5 ("When in the company of the gods")   377
    6 ("In me (the worm) clearly")   377
    8 ("So we reveal our status")   378

SIEGFRIED SASSOON (1886–1967)   379
To His Dead Body   381
"Blighters"   381
The Rear-Guard   382
Dreamers   382
The Fathers   383
The Investiture   383
Repression of War Experience   384
In the National Gallery   384
At Max Gate   385

ROBINSON JEFFERS (1887–1962)   385
Phenomena   388
Shine, Perishing Republic   388
Fawn's Foster-Mother   389
Hurt Hawks   389
Evening Ebb   390
Shane O'Neill's Cairn   390
New Mexican Mountain   391
A Little Scraping   391
Rock and Hawk   392
Ave Caesar   393
Gray Weather   393
The Purse-Seine   393
O Lovely Rock   394
Shiva   395
Watch the Lights Fade   395
But I Am Growing Old and Indolent   396

EDWIN MUIR (1887–1959)   396
Ballad of Hector in Hades   398
Variations on a Time Theme
    III ("A child in Adam's field I dreamed away")   399

IV ("Now at the road's quick turn")   400
VII ("Ransomed from darkness and released in Time")   401
The Mythical Journey   401
The Refugees   402
The Wheel   403
The Three Mirrors   404
The Labyrinth   405
The Absent   407
One Foot in Eden   407
The Horses   408

EDITH SITWELL (1887–1964)   409
Aubade   412
Country Dance   413
Four in the Morning   414
Still Falls the Rain   415
The Poet Laments the Coming of Old Age   416
The Canticle of the Rose   417

MARIANNE MOORE (1887–1972)   418
The Fish   420
Poetry   421
The Monkeys   422
Critics and Connoisseurs   423
A Grave   424
The Steeple-Jack   424
The Pangolin   426
What Are Years?   428
He 'Digesteth Harde Yron'   429
Spenser's Ireland   431

JOHN CROWE RANSOM (1888–1974)   432
Bells for John Whiteside's Daughter   435
Here Lies a Lady   435
Judith of Bethulia   436
Philomela   437
Captain Carpenter   438
Piazza Piece   439
Blue Girls   440
Janet Waking   440
Dead Boy   441
The Equilibrists   442
Painted Head   443
Master's in the Garden Again   444

T. S. ELIOT (1888–1965)   445
The Love Song of J. Alfred Prufrock   449
Whispers of Immortality   452
Sweeney Among the Nightingales   453
Gerontion   455
The Waste Land   457

Ash Wednesday
    III ("At the first turning of the second stair")   471
Little Gidding   472

CONRAD AIKEN (1889–1973)   479
  Senlin: A Biography
    Part II
      2 ("It is morning, Senlin says, and in the morning")   480
  Priapus and the Pool
    III ("When trout swim down Great Ormond Street")   481
  Preludes for Memnon
    II ("Two coffees in the Español, the last")   482
    LVI ("Rimbaud and Verlaine, precious pair of poets")   483
  Hatteras Calling   484
  Dear Uncle Stranger   484
  Summer   485
  Herman Melville   485
  Morning Dialogue   486

CLAUDE McKAY (1890–1948)   488
  The Tropics in New York   489
  If We Must Die   489
  America   489
  The Harlem Dancer   490
  The White City   490

EDNA ST. VINCENT MILLAY (1892–1950)   490
  First Fig   492
  Recuerdo   492
  Grown-Up   493
  Dirge without Music   493
  The Plum Gatherer   493
  [Love Is Not All: It Is Not Meat nor Drink]   494
  [Hearing Your Words, and Not a Word Among Them]   494
  [Oh, Sleep Forever in the Latmian Cave]   494
  The Return   495
  To a Calvinist in Bali   495

ARCHIBALD MacLEISH (1892–1982)   496
  L'An Trentiesme de Mon Eage   498
  The End of the World   498
  Memorial Rain   499
  You, Andrew Marvell   500
  Seafarer   501
  Conquistador
    Prologue   501
  You Also, Gaius Valerius Catullus   503

HUGH MacDIARMID (C. M. Grieve) (1892–1978)   504
  The Sauchs in the Reuch Heuch Hauch   506
  I Heard Christ Sing   506

Crowdieknowe   508
In the Pantry   509
Cloudburst and Soaring Moon   509
Parley of Beasts   510
O Wha's the Bride?   510
Harry Semen   511
Another Epitaph on an Army of Mercenaries   512
British Leftish Poetry, 1930–40   513

WILFRED OWEN (1893–1918)   513
Strange Meeting   515
Greater Love   516
Anthem for Doomed Youth   516
Exposure   517
The Show   518
Dulce et Decorum Est   519
Futility   519
Disabled   520
Mental Cases   521

HERBERT READ (1893–1968)   522
The Execution of Cornelius Vane   523
The Well of Life   526

E. E. CUMMINGS (1894–1962)   526
[All in green went my love riding]   529
[O sweet spontaneous]   530
[the Cambridge ladies who live in furnished souls]   530
[i was siting in mcsorley's]   531
[a man who had fallen among thieves]   532
[(ponder,darling,these busted statues]   532
[come, gaze with me upon this dome]   533
[it is so long since my heart has been with yours]   534
[i sing of Olaf glad and big]   534
[Space being(don't forget to remember)Curved]   535
[little joe gould has lost his teeth and doesn't know where]   536
[you shall above all things be glad and young]   536
[the way to hump a cow is not]   536
[my father moved through dooms of love]   537
[a salesman is an it that stinks Excuse]   539
[plato told]   539
[for prodigal read generous]   540
[why from this her and him]   540
[but]   541

JEAN TOOMER (1894–1967)   541
Reapers   543
November Cotton Flower   543
Georgia Dusk   543
Her Lips Are Copper Wire   544

ROBERT GRAVES (1895–   )   544
Rocky Acres   546
The Pier-Glass   547
Children of Darkness   548
The Cool Web   548
Lost Acres   549
The Legs   549
Ogres and Pygmies   550
Ulysses   551
Down, Wanton, Down!   552
Sick Love   552
The Devil's Advice to Story-Tellers   552
Recalling War   553
To Juan at the Winter Solstice   554
The Persian Version   556
The Blue-Fly   556
My Name and I   557
The Second-Fated   558

DAVID JONES (1895–1974)   559
In Parenthesis
Part 4. King Pellam's Launde (lines 1–33)   561
Part 7. The Five Unmistakable Marks (lines 283–413)   562
The Anathémata
Part III. Angle-Land   565

AUSTIN CLARKE (1896–1974)   570
The Young Woman of Beare   571
Night and Morning   576
Penal Law   577

HART CRANE (1899–1933)   577
Legend   579
Black Tambourine   580
My Grandmother's Love Letters   580
Praise for an Urn   581
Chaplinesque   582
Repose of Rivers   583
Passage   583
The Wine Menagerie   584
For the Marriage of Faustus and Helen   586
At Melville's Tomb   589
Voyages   590
The Bridge
Proem: To Brooklyn Bridge   594
Ave Maria   596
The River   598
O Carib Isle!   602
Royal Palm   603
To Emily Dickinson   603
The Broken Tower   604

ALLEN TATE (1899–1979)   605
   Mr. Pope   607
   Ode to the Confederate Dead   607
   The Subway   610
   The Oath   611
   The Wolves   611
   Last Days of Alice   612
   Aeneas at Washington   613
   Sonnets at Christmas   614

BASIL BUNTING (1900–   )   615
   [Darling of Gods and Men, Beneath the Gliding Stars]   616
   The Orotava Road   617
   On the Fly-Leaf of Pound's Cantos   618
   Briggflatts
      IV ("Grass caught in willow . . .")   618

YVOR WINTERS (1900–1968)   620
   The Rows of Cold Trees   622
   The Castle of Thorns   622
   The Slow Pacific Swell   623
   The Grave   623
   On Teaching the Young   624
   John Sutter   624
   Sir Gawain and the Green Knight   625
   Time and the Garden   626

LAURA RIDING (1901–   )   627
   The Map of Places   628
   Opening of Eyes   628
   With the Face   629
   Auspice of Jewels   630
   Because of Clothes   631
   The Forgiven Past   632

LANGSTON HUGHES (1902–1967)   633
   The Negro Speaks of Rivers   634
   The Weary Blues   635
   Brass Spittoons   636
   Fire   636
   Sylvester's Dying Bed   637
   Morning After   638
   50–50   638
   Madam's Past History   639
   Late Last Night   639
   Catch   640
   Theme for English B   640

STEVIE SMITH (1902–1971)   641
   Not Waving but Drowning   642
   Was He Married?   642
   Was It Not Curious?   643

Admire Cranmer! 644
Exeat 644
To Carry the Child 645

COUNTEE CULLEN (1903–1946) 646
Yet Do I Marvel 647
Incident 647
Heritage 647

WILLIAM PLOMER (1903–1973) 650
The Scorpion 651
The Widow's Plot: or, She Got What Was Coming to Her 652
Father and Son: 1939 654
In the Snake Park 656

LOUIS ZUKOFSKY (1904–1978) 657
[Tall and Singularly Dark You Pass Among the Breakers] 658
[Ask of the Sun] 658
[In Arizona] 659
[For You I Have Emptied the Meaning] 659
Catullus viii 660
Light
  2 ("A house where every") 660
  4 ("These are not my sentiments") 661

RICHARD EBERHART (1904–   ) 661
The Groundhog 663
"Mysticism Has Not the Patience to Wait for God's
    Revelation" 664
The Fury of Aerial Bombardment 665
Analogue of Unity in Multeity 665
Kaire 666
A New England Bachelor 667

CECIL DAY LEWIS (1904–1972) 667
Do Not Expect Again 669
Two Songs 670
Reconciliation 671
The Double Vision 671
Almost Human 672
Sheepdog Trials in Hyde Park 672

PATRICK KAVANAGH (1904–1967) 673
Tinker's Wife 674
Inniskeen Road: July Evening 675
The Great Hunger
  I ("Clay is the word and clay is the flesh") 675
Canal Bank Walk 677
Come Dance with Kitty Stobling 678
In Memory of My Mother 678
Prelude 679
I Had a Future 680
Lecture Hall 681

ROBERT PENN WARREN (1905–   )   682
  History   684
  Revelation   686
  Bearded Oaks   687
  Mexico Is a Foreign Country: Four Studies in Naturalism
    IV. The Mango on the Mango Tree   688
  Promises
    VIII. Founding Fathers, Nineteenth-Century Style, Southeast
      U.S.A.   689
  Notes on a Life to Be Lived
    II. Small White House   691
    III. Blow, West Wind   692
    X. Ways of Day   692
  Penological Study: Southern Exposure
    3. Wet Hair: If Now His Mother Should Come   692

STANLEY KUNITZ (1905–   )   693
  Father and Son   694
  The Last Picnic   695
  The War Against the Trees   695
  A Spark of Laurel   696
  River Road   697

KENNETH REXROTH (1905–   )   698
  Vitamins and Roughage   700
  Lyell's Hypothesis Again   700
  The Great Canzon   702
  The Bad Old Days   703
  Proust's Madeleine   704
  The Wheel Revolves   704

JOHN BETJEMAN (1906–   )   705
  The Arrest of Oscar Wilde at the Cadogan Hotel   706
  An Incident in the Early Life of Ebenezer Jones, Poet, 1828   707
  On a Potrait of a Deaf Man   709

SAMUEL BECKETT (1906–   )   710
  Whoroscope   711
  Enueg II   714
  What Would I Do Without This World Faceless Incurious   715

VERNON WATKINS (1906–1967)   716
  Ballad of the Three Coins   716
  Waterfalls   719
  A True Picture Restored   720

WILLIAM EMPSON (1906–   )   724
  To an Old Lady   725
  Villanelle   726
  Legal Fiction   727
  This Last Pain   727

Bacchus   728
Ignorance of Death   732
Missing Dates   733

W. H. AUDEN (1907–1973)   734
The Letter   736
Prologue   736
The Wanderer   737
Our Hunting Fathers   738
Who's Who   738
[Fish in the Unruffled Lakes]   739
Lullaby   739
Musée des Beaux Arts   740
Our Bias   741
In Memory of W. B. Yeats   741
New Year Letter (lines 1651–84)   743
In Praise of Limestone   744

LINCOLN KIRSTEIN (1907–   )   746
Fall In   747
Foresight   748
Vaudeville   748
Das Schloss   749
Bath   751

THEODORE ROETHKE (1908–1963)   752
Open House   753
"Long Live the Weeds"   753
Epidermal Macabre   754
Cuttings   754
Cuttings (later)   754
My Papa's Waltz   755
Dolor   755
The Minimal   755
Four for Sir John Davies   756
The Waking   758
Frau Bauman, Frau Schmidt, and Frau Schwartze   759
Words for the Wind   759
I Knew a Woman   762
The Exorcism   762
The Young Girl   763
Wish for a Young Wife   763
The Chums   764
Heard in a Violent Ward   764
In a Dark Time   764

A. D. HOPE (1907–   )   765
The Bed   766
Observation Car   767
The Lingam and the Yoni   768
Imperial Adam   769

LOUIS MacNEICE (1907–1963)   770
  Wolves   772
  Snow   772
  Nature Morte   773
  An Eclogue for Christmas   773
  Bagpipe Music   776
  Carrickfergus   777
  The Sunlight on the Garden   778
  Brother Fire   779
  The Libertine   780
  Mahabalipuram   780
  Variation on Heraclitus   782
  Bad Dream   783
  This Is the Life   784

RICHARD WRIGHT (1908–1960)   784
  I Have Seen Black Hands   785
  Between the World and Me   787
  Four Haiku   788

STEPHEN SPENDER (1909–   )   788
  The Funeral   789
  Icarus   790
  Rough   790
  What I Expected   791
  The Express   792
  The Landscape near an Aerodrome   792
  The Pylons   793
  Not Palaces   793
  Perhaps   794
  Hoelderlin's Old Age   795
  The Coward   795
  Polar Exploration   796
  One More New Botched Beginning   797

W. R. RODGERS (1909–1969)   798
  The Swan   799
  Christ Walking on the Water   800
  Armagh   801

CHARLES OLSON (1910–1970)   802
  The Maximus Poems
    I, Maximus of Gloucester, to You   805
    Maximus, to Gloucester (Letter 2)   808
    The Songs of Maximus
      1 ("Colored pictures")   810
      2 ("all")   811
  A Newly Discovered 'Homeric' Hymn   811
  Variations Done for Gerald Van De Wiele   812

ELIZABETH BISHOP (1911–1979)   815
  The Man-Moth   816

The Unbeliever   817
The Monument   817
The Fish   819
Over 2000 Illustrations and a Complete Concordance   821
Brazil, January 1, 1502   822
The Armadillo   823
Some Dreams They Forgot   824

JOSEPHINE MILES (1911–   )   825
On Inhabiting an Orange   826
Made Shine   826
Preliminary to Classroom Lecture   826
So Graven   827
Gypsy   827
Forecast   827
Bounty   828
Belief   828
Reason   828
Tally   829
[The Entrepreneur Chicken Shed His Tail Feathers, Surplus]   829
[As Difference Blends into Identity]   830

J. V. CUNNINGHAM (1911–   )   830
The Phoenix   831
The Chase   832
To the Reader   832
Elegy for a Cricket   833
For a College Yearbook   833
The Aged Lover Discourses in the Flat Style   833
To What Strangers, What Welcome
    I ("I drive westward. Tumble and loco weed")   834

ROY FULLER (1912–   )   834
Death   835
The Barber   835
The Giraffes   836
Shore Leave Lorry   837
Crustaceans   837
Autobiography of a Lungworm   838

BROTHER ANTONINUS (William Everson) (1912–   )   839
Year's End   840
The Raid   840
What Birds Were There   841

KARL SHAPIRO (1913–   )   843
The Dome of Sunday   844
The Fly   845
Poet   846
V-Letter   848
The Alphabet   850
Lower the Standard: That's My Motto   850

ROBERT HAYDEN (1913–1980)   851
  The Ballad of Sue Ellen Westerfield 851
  Witch Doctor 852
  Those Winter Sundays 854
  Middle Passage 854
  " 'Mystery Boy' Looks for Kin in Nashville" 859

DELMORE SCHWARTZ (1913–1966)   859
  In the Naked Bed, in Plato's Cave 861
  Far Rockaway 862
  For the One Who Would Take Man's Life in His Hands 863
  Dogs Are Shakespearean, Children Are Strangers 863
  The Heavy Bear Who Goes with Me 864
  The Winter Twilight, Glowing Black and Gold 865
  The Mind Is an Ancient and Famous Capital 866

DUDLEY RANDALL (1914–   )   866
  Roses and Revolutions 867
  A Different Image 868
  Ballad of Birmingham 868
  Booker T. and W. E. B. 869
  Old Witherington 870
  George 871
  Pacific Epitaphs
    New Georgia 871
    Palawan 871
    Espiritu Santu 872
    Bougainville 872
    Vella Vella 872
    Borneo 872

WELDON KEES (1914–1955)   872
  Midnight 873
  Robinson 873
  River Song 874
  Round 875
  A Distance from the Sea 875

RANDALL JARRELL (1914–1965)   877
  90 North 879
  The Death of the Ball Turret Gunner 879
  Eighth Air Force 880
  A Girl in a Library 880
  A Game at Salzburg 883
  Next Day 884
  Woman · 886
  Thinking of the Lost World 889

JOHN BERRYMAN (1914–1972)   891
  The Ball Poem 893
  Homage to Mistress Bradstreet (lines 1–32, 137–176) 894
  A Professor's Song 896

The Dream Songs
   14 ("Life, friends is boring. We must not say so")   897
   16 ("Henry's pelt was put on sundry walls")   897
   75 ("Turning it over, considering, like a madman')   898
   76 Henry's Confession   898
   149 ("The world is gradually becoming a place")   899
   312 ("I have moved to Dublin to have it out with you")   899
Sonnet 25   900
Of Suicide   900
Henry's Understanding   901

DYLAN THOMAS (1914–1953)   901
  The Force That Through the Green Fuse Drives the Flower   903
  The Hand That Signed the Paper   904
  And Death Shall Have No Dominion   904
  Altarwise by Owl-Light
     I   ("Altarwise by owl-light in the half-way house")   905
     II   ("Death is all metaphors, shape in one history")   905
     V   ("And from the windy West came two-gunned
          Gabriel")   906
     VIII ("This was the crucifixion on the mountain")   906
     IX   ("From the oracular archives and the parchment")   906
     X   ("Let the tale's sailor from a Christian voyage")   907
  When All My Five and Country Senses See   907
  'If My Head Hurt a Hair's Foot'   908
  Twenty-Four Years   908
  A Refusal to Mourn the Death, by Fire, of a Child in London   909
  In My Craft or Sullen Art   909
  Fern Hill   910
  Do Not Go Gentle into That Good Night   911

JOHN MALCOLM BRINNIN (1916–)   912
  Hotel Paradiso e Commerciale   912
  Roethke Plain   913
  John Without Heaven   916

THEODORE WEISS (1916–)   917
  This Narrow Stage   917
  The Fire at Alexandria   918
  The Web   919
  Clothes Maketh the Man   920
  The Ultimate Antientropy   921
  A Sow's Ear   922

ROBERT LOWELL (1917–1977)   924
  Colloquy in Black Rock   927
  The Quaker Graveyard in Nantucket   928
  As a Plane Tree by the Water   931
  After the Surprising Conversions   932
  Falling Asleep over the Aeneid   933
  To Delmore Schwartz   935
  Sailing Home from Rapallo   936
  "To Speak of Woe That Is in Marriage"   937

Skunk Hour   938
For the Union Dead   939
The Old Flame   941
Alfred Corning Clark   942
T. S. Eliot   943
Ezra Pound   943
Robert Frost   944
The Picture   944

GWENDOLYN BROOKS (1917–   )   945
A Song in the Front Yard   945
Sadie and Maud   946
Of De Witt Williams on His Way to Lincoln Cemetery   946
The Vacant Lot   947
The Lovers of the Poor   947
A Penitent Considers Another Coming of Mary   949
Of Robert Frost   950
Boy Breaking Glass   950
The Blackstone Rangers   951

ROBERT CONQUEST (1917–   )   953
The Rokeby Venus   954
By Rail Through Istria   954
Near the Death of Ovid   955
Art and Civilization   956

MARGARET AVISON (1918–   )   957
Tennis   957
The Two Selves   958
For Tinkers Who Travel on Foot   958

A. W. PURDY (1918–   )   959
Girl   960
Dead Seal   961

ROBERT DUNCAN (1919–   )   962
An African Elegy   964
The Ballad of Mrs Noah   966
Poetry, a Natural Thing   968
At Christmas   969
Persephone   969
Passage over Water   970
What I Saw   971

WILLIAM MEREDITH (1919–   )   971
To the Thoughtful Reader   972
Traveling Boy   972
On Falling Asleep by Firelight   973
Bachelor   973
Battle Problem   974
The Couple Overhead   974
Consequences   975
Last Things   976

LAWRENCE FERLINGHETTI (1919?–   )   978
[In Goya's Greatest Scenes We Seem to See]   979
[Sometime During Eternity]   980
[In Golden Gate Park That Day]   981
[Frightened]   982

EDWIN HONIG (1919–   )   983
As a Great Prince   983
Tête-à-Tête   984
Now, My Usefulness Over   984
November Through a Giant Copper Beech   984
Some Knots   985

DAVID WRIGHT (1920–   )   985
An Invocation to the Goddess   986
Monologue of a Deaf Man   987
Kleomedes   988
Grasmere Sonnets   990

HOWARD NEMEROV (1920–   )   991
The Brief Journey West   992
The Scales of the Eyes
    XII ("In the water cave, below the root")   993
I Only Am Escaped Alone to Tell Thee   993
The Goose Fish   994
The Sparrow in the Zoo   995
Brainstorm   995
The Icehouse in Summer   996
Make Love Not War   997
Style   998
The May Day Dancing   999

RICHARD WILBUR (1921–   )   1000
Cigales   1002
The Pardon   1002
Epistemology   1003
Grasse: The Olive Trees   1003
Still, Citizen Sparrow   1004
The Death of a Toad   1005
Ceremony   1005
"A World Without Objects Is a Sensible Emptiness"   1006
Love Calls Us to the Things of This World   1006
Pangloss's Song   1007
A Hole in the Floor   1008
Playboy   1009

KINGSLEY AMIS (1922–   )   1010
A Dream of Fair Women   1011
Against Romanticism   1012
An Ever-Fixed Mark   1013

PHILIP LARKIN (1922–   )   1014
[So Through That Unripe Day You Bore Your Head]   1015

Church Going   1015
Myxomatosis   1016
Toads   1017
Faith Healing   1017
The Whitsun Weddings   1018
Sunny Prestatyn   1020
Dockery and Son   1020
[Waiting for Breakfast, While She Brushed Her Hair]   1022

ANTHONY HECHT (1923–   )   1022
La Condition Botanique   1023
Birdwatchers of America   1026
"More Light! More Light!"   1026
"It Out-Herods Herod. Pray You Avoid It."   1027

JAMES DICKEY (1923–   )   1028
The Performance   1030
The Heaven of Animals   1031
Chenille   1032
Buckdancer's Choice   1034
The Sheep Child   1034

ALAN DUGAN (1923–   )   1036
Love Song: I and Thou   1037
Poem ("The person who can do")   1038
Funeral Oration for a Mouse   1038
How We Heard the Name   1039
Tribute to Kafka for Someone Taken   1040
For Masturbation   1040
Fabrication of Ancestors   1040
Plague of Dead Sharks   1041
Let Heroes Account to Love   1041
Elegy for a Puritan Conscience   1042
On Rape Unattempted   1042
A Trial   1043

LOUIS SIMPSON (1923–   )   1043
The Man Who Married Magdalene   1045
The Green Shepherd   1045
In California   1047
The Morning Light   1048
A Story About Chicken Soup   1048
The Troika   1049
My Father in the Night Commanding No   1049
American Poetry   1051
After Midnight   1051

DANNIE ABSE (1923–   )   1051
Portrait of a Marriage   1052
The Second Coming   1053
The Victim of Aulis   1053
Duality   1055